HOW TO ESCAPE THE MATRIX IN THIS LIFE

RONAK S. KARELIYA.

Made with ♥ on the Notion Press Platform
www.notionpress.com

For

My Parents (Bhavna Kareliya) and (Shailesh Kareliya),who teach me,

MY elder Sister(Mahek Kareliya),who guides me,

MY Idiol who inspire me.

Contents

Author Bio

Ronak Kareliya is a young and inspiring author who has written the transformative book, "A Guide to Escaping the Matrix." At a young age, Ronak discovered his passion for personal growth and development, which led him to delve deeply into the spiritual teachings and practices of various traditions.

In "A Guide to Escaping the Matrix," Ronak shares his personal journey of transformation and offers practical tools and insights to help readers break free from limiting beliefs and patterns of behavior. His approach is grounded in mindfulness and self-awareness, helping young readers to cultivate a deeper connection to themselves and the world around them.

As a teen boy who has already accomplished so much, Ronak is a true inspiration to his peers and to people of all ages. His message of empowerment and possibility is one that resonates with young people who are searching for meaning and purpose in their lives.

Through his book and his speaking engagements, Ronak encourages young people to embrace their unique gifts and talents and to live authentically and courageously. His passion for personal growth and development is contagious, and he is a shining example of what is possible when we believe in ourselves and our ability to create a life of purpose and meaning.

About Book

"A Guide to Escaping the Matrix" is a transformative and eye-opening book that takes readers on a journey of self-discovery and enlightenment. Written by a RONAK KARELIYA the author, this book offers a powerful and practical roadmap to help readers break free from the limiting beliefs and behaviors that keep them stuck in the matrix of their own making.

Drawing on a wealth of spiritual wisdom and practical insights, "A Guide to Escaping the Matrix" provides readers with a step-by-step guide to shedding their old patterns of thought and behavior, and embracing a new, more empowered way of living. From cultivating mindfulness and developing a deeper connection to the present moment, to learning how to identify and overcome self-limiting beliefs, this book is a comprehensive resource for anyone seeking to live a more fulfilling and authentic life.

Whether you're feeling stuck in a dead-end job, struggling with a difficult relationship, or simply seeking greater clarity and purpose in your life, "A Guide to Escaping the Matrix" is an essential read. Packed with actionable advice and inspiring stories of transformation, this book is a powerful tool for anyone ready to break free from the constraints of their old way of thinking and step into a life of greater possibility and potential.

CHAPTER ONE

Recognizing The Matrix

1.1] Define the matrix and explain how its affect our lives.

The Matrix is a concept, story, and film trilogy that explores a dystopian future in which humans are trapped inside a simulated reality created by machines. The simulated reality, called the Matrix, appears to be a physical world, but it is actually a computer-generated simulation that feeds sensory input to the human brain.

The Matrix affects our lives in several ways. First and foremost, it serves as a metaphor for the various ways in which we may feel trapped or limited by external forces. Whether it is societal norms, cultural expectations, or personal beliefs, we may feel as though our lives are constrained by factors beyond our control.

Secondly, the Matrix highlights the importance of questioning our assumptions and seeking deeper understanding of the world around us. The main character in the movie, Neo, must confront his own preconceptions and learn to see the world in a new way in order to break free from the Matrix.

Finally, the Matrix can also be seen as a commentary on the dangers of technology and our increasing reliance on digital tools and virtual experiences. The film warns of the potential for technology to be used to control and manipulate people, and urges us to remain vigilant and aware of these risks.

Overall, the Matrix serves as a powerful symbol of the human struggle for freedom, self-discovery, and meaning, and can inspire us to question our own assumptions and strive for a more authentic and fulfilling existence.

1.2] Example of how matrix operates in different areas of life, such as work, reletionship ,and media.

The concept of the Matrix can be applied to various areas of life, including work, relationships, and media. Here are some examples of how the Matrix operates in these areas:

Work: In the context of work, the Matrix can be seen as the norms and expectations that define what success looks like and how we should pursue it. For example, we may feel pressure to climb the corporate ladder, even if it means sacrificing our personal values or relationships. The Matrix of work can also involve the sense of being trapped in a job or career that doesn't align with our passions or purpose.

Relationships: In the realm of relationships, the Matrix can refer to the societal expectations and cultural norms that dictate how we should interact with others. For example, we may feel pressure to conform to certain gender roles or to pursue a conventional romantic relationship, even if it doesn't feel authentic to us. The Matrix of relationships can also involve the sense of being trapped in toxic or unfulfilling relationships that limit our growth and potential.

Media: In the context of media, the Matrix can be seen as the narratives and messages that shape our beliefs and perspectives. For example, the media may promote a certain ideal of beauty or success that can be limiting and oppressive. The Matrix of media can also involve the sense of being trapped in an echo chamber or filter bubble, where we are only exposed to ideas and opinions that confirm our existing beliefs.

Overall, the Matrix operates in various areas of life by defining and shaping our sense of what is possible and desirable. By becoming aware of the Matrix and questioning our assumptions and beliefs, we can break free from limiting patterns and pursue a more authentic and fulfilling life.

CHAPTER TWO

Understanding Your Programming

2.1] How we are programmed by society, family and culture.

As humans, we are social creatures who are deeply influenced by the people and cultures around us. From a young age, we are programmed by society, family, and culture to think and act in certain ways. Here are some ways in which we are programmed by these external factors:

Society: Society is a powerful force that shapes our beliefs, values, and behavior. We are socialized to conform to social norms and expectations, such as the idea that we should work hard, be successful, and conform to certain gender roles. Society also influences the way we see ourselves and others, and can create stereotypes and biases that affect our perceptions and actions.

Family: Our families play a crucial role in our development and programming. From a young age, we are taught by our parents and caregivers how to think and act in the world. We learn our values, beliefs, and behavior patterns from our family members, and often adopt their attitudes and beliefs as our own.

Culture: Culture refers to the shared beliefs, values, customs, and practices of a particular group of people. Our cultural background can influence everything from our language and food preferences to our attitudes and beliefs about the world. Culture also shapes our sense of identity and can influence our behavior in social situations.

All of these external factors can have a powerful impact on our programming, shaping the way we see ourselves and others, the choices we make, and the opportunities we pursue. While programming can be beneficial in some ways, it can also be limiting and oppressive. By becoming aware of our programming and questioning our assumptions and beliefs, we can break free from limiting patterns and live a more authentic and fulfilling life.

2.2] The role of conditioning and belief in shaping our reality

Our conditioning and beliefs play a crucial role in shaping our reality. From a young age, we are exposed to a wide range of experiences, messages, and social cues that shape our beliefs and attitudes about the world. These beliefs and attitudes then shape our perceptions and actions, influencing how we interact with others and the world around us. Here are some ways in which conditioning and belief shape our reality:

1- Perception: Our beliefs and conditioning influence how we perceive the world around us. For example, if we believe that the world is a dangerous place, we may be more likely to see danger in situations that others perceive as safe.

2- Interpretation: Our beliefs and conditioning also shape how we interpret events and experiences. For example, if we believe that failure is bad, we may interpret setbacks as evidence of our own inadequacy, rather than as an opportunity for growth.

3- Behavior: Our beliefs and conditioning also influence our behavior, determining the actions we take and the choices we make. For example, if we believe that hard work is the key to success, we may work long hours and sacrifice our health and relationships in pursuit of our goals.

4- Reality creation: Our beliefs and conditioning also play a role in creating our reality. For example, if we believe that we are not worthy of love, we may struggle to form and maintain healthy relationships.

Overall, our conditioning and beliefs shape our reality by influencing our perceptions, interpretations, behavior, and reality creation. By becoming aware of our conditioning and beliefs, we can challenge and transform limiting patterns and create a more fulfilling and authentic life.

CHAPTER THREE

Overcoming Fear And Resistance

3.1] Identify common fears and resistance that prevent us from from breaking free

Breaking free from societal norms and programming can be a challenging and uncomfortable process. Here are some common fears and resistance that can prevent us from breaking free:

1- Fear of the unknown: The unknown can be scary, and breaking free from the Matrix often involves stepping outside of our comfort zone and taking risks. We may fear the uncertainty of the future and the possibility of failure or rejection.

2- Fear of judgment: We may worry about what others will think of us if we deviate from the norm. We may fear being judged or criticized by our peers, family, or society at large.

3- Attachment to identity: Our sense of identity is often tied up in the roles we play and the beliefs we hold. Breaking free from the Matrix can involve letting go of these identity markers, which can be scary and disorienting.

4- Lack of support: Breaking free from the Matrix can be a lonely and isolating process, particularly if those around us are not supportive or understanding of our journey.

5- Conditioning: Our programming is deeply ingrained in our minds and bodies, and breaking free can involve overcoming years of conditioning and automatic responses.

These fears and resistance can be powerful obstacles to breaking free from the Matrix, but with awareness and support, we can overcome them and create a more authentic and fulfilling life. It's important to recognize that breaking free is not a one-time event, but an ongoing process that requires courage, persistence, and self-reflection.

3.2] Strategies and techniques to overcome these obstacle of matrix

Breaking free from the Matrix can be a challenging and uncomfortable process, but there are strategies and techniques that can help us overcome these obstacles. Here are some techniques that can be helpful:

1- Self-awareness: The first step to breaking free from the Matrix is to become aware of our conditioning and beliefs. This can involve reflecting on our past experiences and identifying the messages and social cues that have shaped our beliefs and attitudes. Journaling, therapy, and mindfulness practices can be helpful in developing self-awareness.

2- Questioning assumptions: Once we are aware of our conditioning and beliefs, we can begin to question the assumptions and beliefs that no longer serve us. We can ask ourselves questions like "Is this belief true?" and "Where did this belief come from?" This can help us to challenge and transform limiting patterns.

3- Developing a growth mindset: Developing a growth mindset, which involves embracing challenges, learning from failure, and believing in our own ability to grow and change, can be helpful in breaking free from the Matrix. We can cultivate a growth mindset by focusing on learning and growth rather than success and achievement.

4- Seeking support: Breaking free from the Matrix can be a lonely and isolating process, so it's important to seek support from others who are on a similar journey. This can involve joining a community or support group, finding a mentor, or seeking out supportive friends and family members.

5- Taking action: Finally, breaking free from the Matrix requires taking action and stepping outside of our comfort zone. This can involve trying new things, taking risks, and challenging ourselves to do things differently. By taking action, we can create new neural pathways and transform limiting patterns.

Overall, breaking free from the Matrix requires a combination of self-awareness, questioning assumptions, developing a growth mindset, seeking support, and taking action. By using these techniques, we can create a more fulfilling and authentic life.

CHAPTER FOUR

Devloping Inner Awarness

4.1] The importance of self awareness in escaping the matrix

Self-awareness is essential in escaping the Matrix because it allows us to recognize the conditioning and beliefs that have been imposed on us by society, culture, and family. It helps us to understand our own patterns of thinking, feeling, and behaving, and to see how these patterns have been shaped by external influences.

Self-awareness also helps us to identify the parts of ourselves that are authentic and true, and to separate these from the parts that are simply products of our conditioning. By recognizing our conditioning, we can begin to question our assumptions and beliefs, and to develop a more authentic sense of self.

In the process of escaping the Matrix, self-awareness also allows us to recognize and work through our fears and resistance. We can see how our conditioning has created these fears and resistance, and we can begin to challenge and transform them.

Overall, self-awareness is a key component in escaping the Matrix because it allows us to recognize our conditioning, question our assumptions and beliefs, and develop a more authentic sense of self.

4.2] Tools and exercises to develop inner self-awareness

There are several tools and exercises that can help develop inner self-awareness, including:

1- Meditation: Meditation is a powerful tool for developing self-awareness. It involves focusing the mind and becoming present in the moment. Regular meditation practice can help to quiet the mind, increase focus and concentration, and improve emotional regulation.

2- Journaling: Journaling is another effective way to develop self-awareness. Writing down our thoughts and feelings can help us to identify patterns and beliefs that may be limiting us. It can also be helpful to reflect on our experiences and to identify the lessons we have learned.

3- Mindfulness: Mindfulness is the practice of being present in the moment and observing our thoughts and feelings without judgment. It involves developing an awareness of our thoughts and feelings and learning to respond to them in a non-reactive way.

4- Self-reflection: Self-reflection involves taking time to reflect on our experiences and to identify the lessons we have learned. It can be helpful to ask ourselves questions like "What did I learn from this experience?" and "What can I do differently next time?"

5- Therapy: Therapy can be a helpful tool for developing self-awareness. A trained therapist can provide guidance and support as we explore our thoughts, feelings, and beliefs. They can also help us to identify patterns and behaviors that may be holding us back.

Overall, developing self-awareness requires a commitment to ongoing self-reflection and self-exploration. By incorporating tools and exercises like meditation, journaling, mindfulness, self-reflection, and therapy, we can cultivate a deeper understanding of ourselves and develop a more authentic sense of self.

CHAPTER FIVE

Creating A New Reality

Chapter-5

5.1] Create a new reality that aligns with your true self and values.

Creating a new reality that aligns with your true self and values involves a process of self-discovery and transformation. Here are some steps that can help in this process:

1-Identify your values: The first step is to identify your values. Values are the things that are most important to you in life, such as honesty, authenticity, freedom, or creativity. By identifying your values, you can begin to create a vision for the kind of life that aligns with them.

2-Clarify your vision: Once you have identified your values, the next step is to clarify your vision for the future. This involves imagining the kind of life you want to create for yourself, based on your values. What kind of work do you want to do? What kind of relationships do you want to have? What kind of lifestyle do you want to lead?

3-Take action: Creating a new reality requires taking action towards your vision. This may involve making changes in your life, such as changing your career, ending toxic relationships, or moving to a new location. It may also involve developing new skills or habits that support your vision.

4-Embrace discomfort: Creating a new reality can be uncomfortable and challenging. It may involve stepping outside of your comfort zone and taking risks. It's important to embrace discomfort and to recognize that growth and transformation often require us to face our fears and push through resistance.

5-Practice self-care: Finally, creating a new reality requires taking care of yourself. This may involve practicing self-care, such as getting enough sleep, eating well, exercising, and practicing mindfulness. It may also involve seeking support from others, such as a therapist or a supportive community.

Overall, creating a new reality that aligns with your true self and values requires a commitment to ongoing self-discovery and transformation. By identifying your values, clarifying your vision, taking action, embracing discomfort, and practicing self-care, you can create a more authentic and fulfilling life.

5.2] Examples of people who have successfully broken free from the matrix

There are many examples of people who have successfully broken free from the matrix and created lives that align with their true selves and values. Here are a few examples:

1- Oprah Winfrey: Oprah Winfrey is a media mogul, philanthropist, and actress who has overcome significant adversity in her life. She was born into poverty in rural Mississippi and faced abuse and trauma as a child. However, she was able to break free from the limitations of her past and create a successful career in television and media. She is now one of the most influential and powerful women in the world.

2- Nelson Mandela: Nelson Mandela was a South African anti-apartheid revolutionary, political leader, and philanthropist who spent 27 years in prison for his political activism. Despite facing significant challenges, he never lost sight of his vision for a more just and equal society. After his release from prison, he became the first black president of South Africa and worked to dismantle the country's apartheid system.

3- Maya Angelou: Maya Angelou was an American poet, memoirist, and civil rights activist who overcame poverty, trauma, and racism to become one of the most important literary figures of the 20th century. She wrote several autobiographical books, including "I Know Why the Caged Bird Sings," which detailed her experiences growing up in the Jim Crow South. Despite facing significant adversity, she remained committed to her vision for social justice and equality.

4- Eckhart Tolle: Eckhart Tolle is a spiritual teacher and author who has written several books on the power of mindfulness and presence. He struggled with depression and anxiety for many years before experiencing a profound spiritual awakening that transformed his life. He now travels the world teaching others about the power of presence and mindfulness.

5- J.K. Rowling: J.K. Rowling is a British author who overcame significant challenges before becoming one of the most successful writers of all time. She was a single mother living on welfare when she began writing the "Harry Potter" series. Despite facing rejection from multiple publishers, she

persisted and eventually found success. She is now one of the wealthiest women in the world and a major philanthropist.

CHAPTER SIX

Taking Action

6.1] The importance of of taking action to create change

An idea or a dream that you've been thinking about, don't wait - take action today and start creating Taking action is an essential step in creating change in our lives and in the world around us. Without action, our ideas and aspirations remain just that - ideas. Here are a few reasons why taking action is so important:

Action brings clarity: Taking action allows us to test our ideas and gain clarity on what works and what doesn't. It's easy to get caught up in analysis paralysis and never take action, but the only way to truly know if something will work is to try it.

Action creates momentum: Once we start taking action, it becomes easier to keep going. Action creates momentum, and momentum creates more action. As we start to see progress and results, we are more motivated to continue.

Action leads to learning: Taking action allows us to learn from our mistakes and failures. We can't improve if we don't try new things and take risks. By taking action, we gain valuable experience that can help us make better decisions in the future.

Action inspires others: When we take action and create positive change in our lives and in the world, we inspire others to do the same. Our actions can have a ripple effect that reaches far beyond our immediate circle of influence.

Action is empowering: Taking action gives us a sense of control over our lives and our circumstances. It allows us to move from a state of passivity to a state of empowerment. By taking action, we can create the kind of life and world that we want to live in.

In short, taking action is essential for creating change. It allows us to gain clarity, create momentum, learn from our mistakes, inspire others, and feel empowered. So if you have the change you want to see.

6.2] Step and Strategies for taking action and making positive changes in your life

Here are some specific steps and strategies for taking action and making positive changes in your life:

Set clear goals: Start by setting clear goals for what you want to achieve. Be specific and make sure your goals are measurable and achievable.

Break your goals down into smaller steps: Once you have your goals, break them down into smaller, more manageable steps. This will make your goals less overwhelming and easier to achieve.

1. Create a plan: Create a plan for how you will achieve your goals. This can include specific actions you need to take, deadlines you need to meet, and resources you will need to use.

2. Take consistent action: Once you have your plan, take consistent action towards your goals. This means setting aside time each day or each week to work on your goals, even if it's just a small step.

3. Track your progress: Keep track of your progress towards your goals. This will help you stay motivated and make any necessary adjustments to your plan.

4. Hold yourself accountable: Hold yourself accountable for taking action towards your goals. This can mean setting up systems to track your progress or finding an accountability partner who can help you stay on track.

5. Celebrate your successes: Celebrate your successes along the way. This will help keep you motivated and inspire you to keep taking action towards your goals.

Remember, taking action and making positive changes in your life is a process. It takes time and effort, but with the right mindset and strategies, you can achieve your goals and create the life you want to live.

CHAPTER SEVEN

Staying Free

7.1] How to maintain your freedom and continue growing after breaking free from the matrix

Breaking free from the matrix is just the first step towards creating a more fulfilling and authentic life. Once you have broken free, it's important to continue growing and maintaining your freedom. Here are some strategies for doing so:

Stay connected to your values and purpose: Remember why you broke free from the matrix in the first place. Stay connected to your values and purpose, and make sure that your actions align with them.

Keep learning and growing: Just because you've broken free from the matrix doesn't mean you've reached the end of your journey. Keep learning and growing, whether it's through reading, taking courses, or seeking out new experiences.

Surround yourself with supportive people: Surround yourself with people who support your growth and encourage you to be your authentic self. Avoid people who try to pull you back into the matrix or discourage you from pursuing your dreams.

Practice self-care: Taking care of yourself is essential for maintaining your freedom and well-being. Make sure to prioritize self-care practices such as meditation, exercise, and spending time in nature.

Embrace uncertainty and take risks: Breaking free from the matrix often involves taking risks and embracing uncertainty. Don't be afraid to step outside of your comfort zone and try new things.

Set new goals: Once you've achieved your initial goals, set new ones that continue to challenge and inspire you.

Give back to others: Use your newfound freedom to give back to others and make a positive impact in the world. Volunteer your time, donate to charity, or use your skills and expertise to help others.

By staying connected to your values, continuing to learn and grow, surrounding yourself with supportive people, practicing self-care, embracing uncertainty, setting new goals, and giving back to others, you can maintain your freedom and continue to create a fulfilling and authentic life.

7.2] Tips and Advice for saying true to yourself and avoiding the traps of the matrix

Staying true to yourself and avoiding the traps of the matrix can be challenging, but with the right mindset and strategies, it is possible. Here are some tips and advice for staying true to yourself:

Know yourself: Take the time to understand who you are, what you value, and what brings you fulfillment. This will help you stay true to yourself when faced with external pressures or expectations.

Listen to your intuition: Trust your gut instincts and listen to your intuition. This can help guide you towards decisions and actions that are aligned with your true self.

Set boundaries: Establish clear boundaries for yourself and communicate them to others. This can help you avoid being pulled into situations or relationships that don't align with your values.

Practice self-compassion: Be kind and compassionate towards yourself, even when you make mistakes or face challenges. This can help you stay resilient and bounce back from setbacks.

Surround yourself with supportive people: Seek out relationships with people who support and encourage you to be your authentic self. Avoid people who try to manipulate or control you, or who don't respect your boundaries.

Be mindful of media and advertising: Be aware of how media and advertising can influence your thoughts and behavior. Question messages that encourage conformity or that don't align with your values.

Cultivate a growth mindset: Adopt a growth mindset and focus on learning and growing, rather than on achieving external measures of success or validation.

Remember, staying true to yourself and avoiding the traps of the matrix is an ongoing process. It requires self-awareness, self-compassion, and a commitment to growth and authenticity. By practicing these tips and strategies, you can stay true to yourself and create a more fulfilling and authentic life.

Conclusion:

8.1] Recap the main points of the book and emphasize the importance of breaking free from the matrix

The main point of the book is that we are living in a "matrix" - a system of societal conditioning, beliefs, and expectations that can limit our potential and prevent us from living a fulfilling and authentic life. Breaking free from the matrix requires self-awareness, courage, and a commitment to growth and authenticity.

Throughout the book, we discussed how the matrix operates in various areas of life, including work, relationships, and media, and identified common fears and resistance that prevent us from breaking free. We also provided strategies and techniques for overcoming these obstacles, such as cultivating self-awareness, practicing self-compassion, setting boundaries, and staying connected to our values and purpose.

It's important to break free from the matrix because living an inauthentic life can lead to feelings of dissatisfaction, anxiety, and depression. Breaking free allows us to live a more fulfilling and authentic life, aligned with our true self and values. It also allows us to contribute to the world in a more meaningful way, and to make a positive impact on those around us.

In summary, breaking free from the matrix is essential for living a fulfilling and authentic life, and requires self-awareness, courage, and a commitment to growth and authenticity.

8.2] Encouragement and inspiration for readers to take action and create the life they truly want.

If you're feeling stuck or unfulfilled, know that you have the power to create the life you truly want. It may not be easy, but it is possible with effort and commitment. Remember that you are not alone - many people have gone through similar struggles and have come out stronger and happier on the other side.

Start by taking small steps towards your goals. It can be as simple as setting aside time each day to reflect on your values and goals, or taking a class to learn a new skill. Surround yourself with supportive people who encourage and inspire you, and seek out resources that can help you along the way, such as books, podcasts, or coaches.

Remember that it's okay to make mistakes or experience setbacks. The journey to creating the life you want may not be linear, but each step is an opportunity for growth and learning. Practice self-compassion and celebrate your progress, no matter how small.

Finally, trust in yourself and your ability to create the life you truly want. You have the power to make positive changes in your life and to live authentically and fulfillingly. Keep going, and know that a fulfilling and authentic life is within reach.

BY AUTHOR - RONAK KARELIYA

"quotes"

1. "The Matrix is a system, Neo. That system is our enemy. But when you're inside, you look around, what do you see? Businessmen, teachers, lawyers, carpenters. The very minds of the people we are trying to save. But until we do, these people are still a part of that system and that makes them our enemy. You have to understand, most of these people are not ready to be unplugged. And many of them are so inert, so hopelessly dependent on the system, that they will fight to protect it." - Morpheus, The Matrix

2. "The truth will set you free, but first it will piss you off." - Gloria Steinem

3. "You have to let it all go, Neo. Fear, doubt, and disbelief. Free your mind." - Morpheus, The Matrix

4. "To be yourself in a world that is constantly trying to make you something else is the greatest accomplishment." - Ralph Waldo Emerson

5. "The greatest prison people live in is the fear of what other people think." - David Icke

6. "Don't let someone else's opinion of you become your reality." - Les Brown

7. "The more you know yourself, the less you are like anyone else, which makes you unique." - Walt Disney

8. "The only way to deal with fear is to face it head-on." - Unknown

9. "It is not the strongest or the most intelligent who will survive but those who can best manage change." - Charles Darwin

10. "You are not a drop in the ocean. You are the entire ocean in a drop." - Rumi

11. "No dream is too big, and no dreamer is too small." - Turbo

9 798890 022745

Printed by Libri Plureos GmbH in Hamburg,
Germany